Cambridge **Discovery Education**™
▶ INTERACTIVE READERS

Series editor: Bob Hastings

VENICE
THE FLOATING CITY

W0099640

B1

Diane Naughton

CAMBRIDGE
UNIVERSITY PRESS

Discovery
EDUCATION™

CAMBRIDGE
UNIVERSITY PRESS

32 Avenue of the Americas, New York, NY 10013-2473, USA

Cambridge University Press is part of the University of Cambridge.

It furthers the University's mission by disseminating knowledge in the pursuit of education, learning and research at the highest international levels of excellence.

www.cambridge.org
Information on this title: www.cambridge.org/9781107621633

© Cambridge University Press 2014

This publication is in copyright. Subject to statutory exception and to the provisions of relevant collective licensing agreements, no reproduction of any part may take place without the written permission of Cambridge University Press.

First published 2014
3rd printing 2015

Printed in Hong Kong, China, by Golden Cup Printing Company Limited

A catalogue record for this publication is available from the British Library

Library of Congress Cataloging-in-Publication Data

Naughton, Diane.
  Venice : the floating city / Diane Naughton.
     pages cm. — (Cambridge discovery interactive readers)
  ISBN 978-1-107-62163-3 (pbk. : alk. paper)
  1. Venice (Italy)—Juvenile literature. 2. English language—Textbooks for foreign speakers.
  3. Readers (Elementary) I. Title.
DG676.N38 2014
945.'311—dc23

                              2013013703

ISBN 978-1-107-62163-3

Additional resources for this publication at www.cambridge.org

Cambridge University Press has no responsibility for the persistence or accuracy of URLs for external or third-party internet websites referred to in this publication, and does not guarantee that any content on such websites is, or will remain, accurate or appropriate.

Layout services, art direction, book design, and photo research: Q2ABillSMITH GROUP
Editorial services: Hyphen S.A.
Audio production: CityVox, New York
Video production: Q2ABillSMITH GROUP

Contents

Before You Read: Get Ready!

American writer Fran Lebowitz once said, "If you read a lot, nothing is as great as you've imagined. Venice is – Venice is better." Read on and you'll find out why.

Words to Know

Complete the sentences with the correct words.

lagoon   palace   mask   costume   flood

1 A _____ happens when it rains a lot and roads become covered with water.

2 A _____ is a beautiful building where kings and queens often live.

3 A _____ is a set of clothes worn in order to look like someone else – at parties, or by actors in movies and plays.

4 A _____ covers a person's face. It can be funny or frightening.

5 A _____ is an area of seawater separated from the sea by a line of rocks or sand.

? ANALYZE

Venice is on a lagoon. Why would people choose to live somewhere like this?

Words to Know

Read the paragraph. Then complete the definitions with the correct highlighted words.

I love carnival time. We wear costumes and masks and decorate our houses. We have fun in the streets and watch the boats float along the canals. Unfortunately, there has been a big rise in prices recently. Everything is so expensive. But my country does a lot of trade with other countries, so there are lots of jobs.

1 _____ (n): the buying and selling of things

2 _____ (v): stay on top of the water or to move gently in the air

3 _____ (n): a special time of year when there are street parties

4 _____ (v): make something look nicer

5 _____ (v): move up

CHAPTER 1

The History of Venice

BORN OUT OF WAR, RAISED ON TRADE, VENICE HAS BEEN A EUROPEAN **JEWEL** FOR 1500 YEARS.

The story of Venice started when the Germans and the Huns attacked the Roman Empire.[1] Many people ran away from their homes. Some came to a **lagoon** along the Adriatic coast that contained 118 islands. They began building homes and businesses. In 421 CE the floating city of Venice was born.

Venice became politically and **economically** important. Ships doing business between Europe and the Far East often stopped at Venice. It quickly became a busy port[2] and before long, Venice controlled most international **trade**. By the late 13th century, it was the richest city in Europe.

[1]**empire:** a group of countries ruled by a single person or government
[2]**port:** an area of a town next to the water; ships arrive and leave from there

Venice is famous for art. The city had many rich people, powerful families, politicians, and church leaders. They built palaces, public areas, and churches. They paid the best artists, such as Titian and Tintoretto, to decorate their buildings. Venice is also famous for music. The composer[3] Vivaldi was born there.

Marco Polo (1254–1324) also came from Venice. He was one of the first Europeans to go to Mongolia and China. His book, *The Travels of Marco Polo*, was popular all around Europe. Other cities and countries began to trade with the Far East. As a result of this new competition, Venice soon no longer controlled international trade, and it began to lose its economic power.

Marco Polo

----

[3] **composer:** a person who writes music

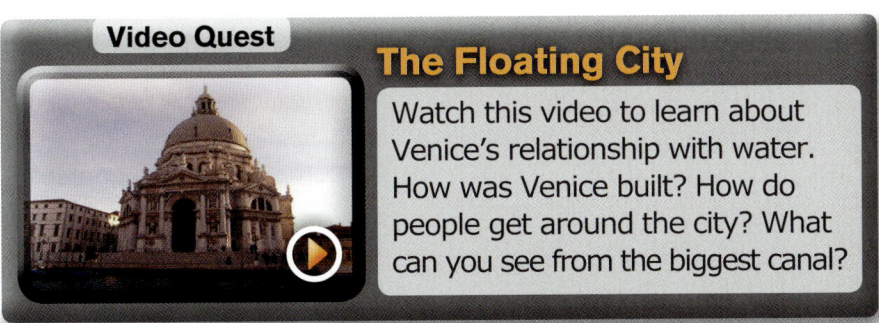

Video Quest

The Floating City

Watch this video to learn about Venice's relationship with water. How was Venice built? How do people get around the city? What can you see from the biggest canal?

CHAPTER 2

The Streets of Venice

VENICE IS ONE OF THE MOST IMPORTANT TOURIST ATTRACTIONS IN THE WORLD.

Venice receives about 50,000 visitors a day. Some want to experience the city's famous art, music, and **architecture**. Others love Venice's modern attractions: fashionable hotels, delicious food, and colorful festivals.

Venice's historical center is small – not much more than five square kilometers. The first thing that visitors notice is that there are no buses or cars. In fact, it is the largest traffic-free city in Europe. To get around, tourists must choose between traveling on foot or on the water, just like people had to do centuries ago.

People who decide to walk may get lost as they try to find their way around the maze[4] of narrow streets. They might find themselves on a street with no way out, or they might want to cross a canal but find that there is no bridge. Despite being small, Venice can be very tiring to get around on foot.

One of the most amazing things about Venice is the way it was built. The lagoon is not very deep. Millions of pieces of wood, called piles, were pushed into the ground under the water. A platform sits on top of these piles, and that is the floor for all the architectural wonders of Venice. Most of the original piles are still there, because wood isn't destroyed by salt water as it is by air. It becomes hard like stone. Tourists in Venice today are sleeping, eating, and walking on top of pieces of wood from the 5th century.

....
[4]**maze:** streets or paths organized in a confusing way

People who choose to travel by boat have many choices and many **routes** they can follow. The Grand Canal is the busiest and biggest of these routes. Just over three kilometers long, it crosses the city center in the shape of a backward letter S. It is between 30 and 70 meters wide, with its widest point next to the *Piazza San Marco* (St. Mark's Square). The other Venetian canals are quite small in comparison. The Grand Canal

is like the main street of other cities, except it has almost no sidewalks. The best way to see the front of the beautiful buildings along the Grand Canal is from a boat.

Boats in Venice are like buses in other cities. The bigger boats are called *vaporetti*, and most of them have seats inside and outside. They can be very slow, however, because they make frequent stops to let passengers on and off. Another possibility is to take a water taxi. This way you can travel quickly and directly to your destination. But have your wallet ready – they can be expensive!

?

ANALYZE

How do you think tourism is good for Venice and the people who live there? How do you think tourism could be a problem?

The most romantic way to see Venice is to ride in a gondola.[5] Gondolas first appeared in the 11th century. They were used by workers to take things from one part of the city to another. By the 17th century, there were 8,000–10,000 beautiful gondolas traveling up and down Venice's canals. Casanova, the famous romantic adventurer, escaped from a Venice prison in 1756 by jumping from a window into a gondola.

Nowadays, there are just over 400 gondolas in Venice. They are most often used to take tourists on pleasure trips, but they are also used for special **civic** celebrations – such as races.

[5]**gondola:** a long, narrow boat typical in Venice; sailed by a gondolier

One of the most famous gondola races takes place every April 25, on St. Mark's Day. Traditionally, gondoliers were always men, but in 2009, after a long fight, Giorgia Boscolo became the first woman gondolier.

The bridges of Venice are wonderful. Some are simple; others are amazing works of art. A local legend[6] says that couples who kiss on a gondola under the *Ponte dei Sospiri*, or Bridge of Sighs,[7] at sunset, will love each other forever. The Bridge of Sighs connects the Doge's Palace to the old prison. Built in 1600, the bridge got its name from Lord Byron, a famous 19th-century English poet. He imagined that prisoners would sigh deeply, enjoying their last chance to see the beauty of Venice.

....

[6] **legend:** a story from a time long ago in the past

[7] **sigh:** the noise you make when you breathe out, often because you are sad

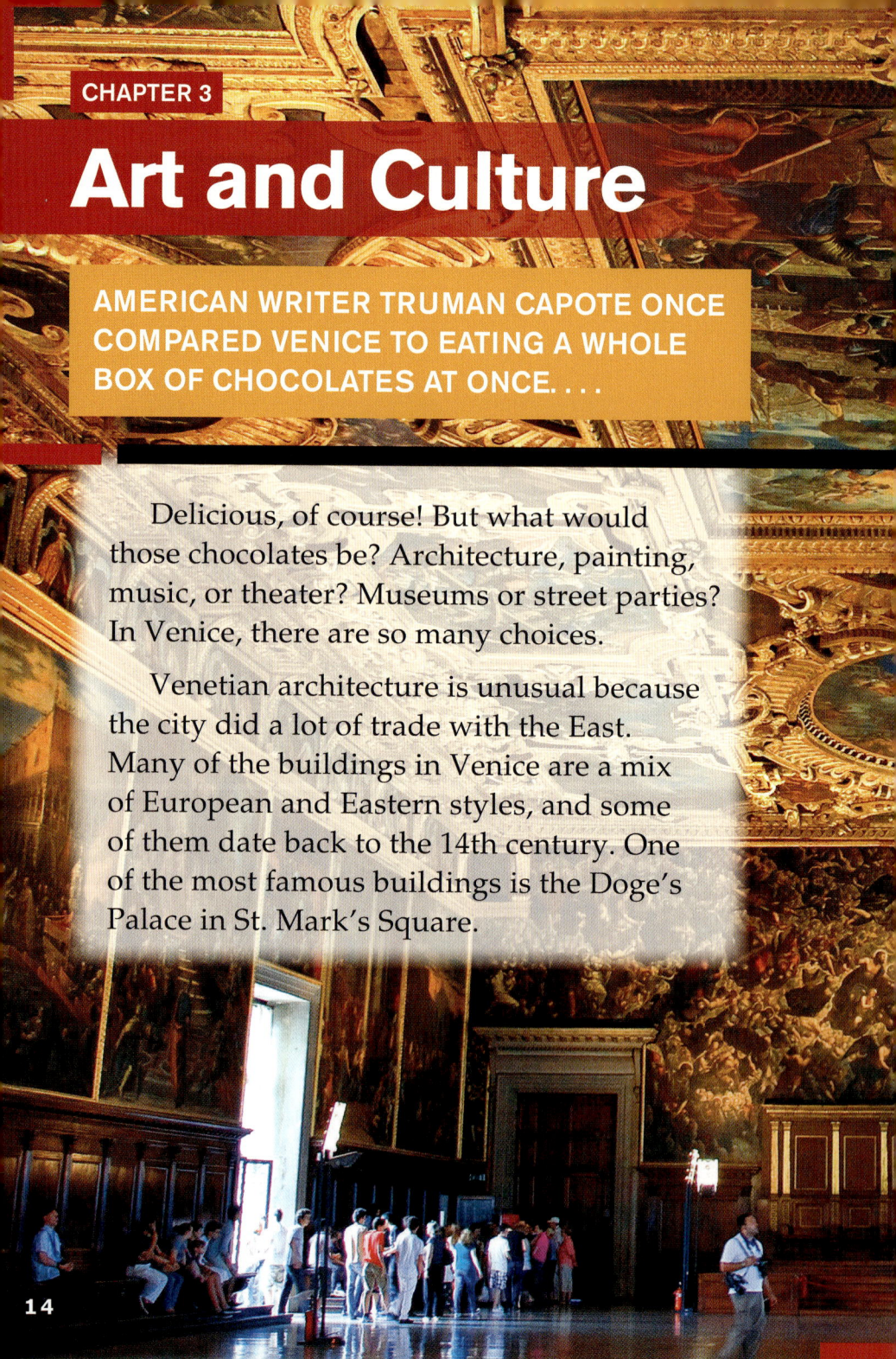

CHAPTER 3

Art and Culture

AMERICAN WRITER TRUMAN CAPOTE ONCE COMPARED VENICE TO EATING A WHOLE BOX OF CHOCOLATES AT ONCE. . . .

Delicious, of course! But what would those chocolates be? Architecture, painting, music, or theater? Museums or street parties? In Venice, there are so many choices.

Venetian architecture is unusual because the city did a lot of trade with the East. Many of the buildings in Venice are a mix of European and Eastern styles, and some of them date back to the 14th century. One of the most famous buildings is the Doge's Palace in St. Mark's Square.

The palace is built mainly in the Gothic style,[8] but with many parts in an Eastern style as well. It used to be home to the civic leaders of Venice, but today the Doge's Palace is a museum.

Although during the 18th century Venice was losing its power as a trading port, it was quickly becoming an important center of fashion. The Venetians loved to decorate the insides of their palaces with great care and attention. Furniture was made by hand and decorated with wooden flowers and angels. There were many mirrors decorated with gold and silver. Colorful pictures were painted on the walls and the ceilings. Beautiful things were brought from foreign countries to make even the simplest house seem like a king's palace.

[8] **Gothic style:** a style of architecture popular in Europe from the 12th to the 16th century

APPLY

If Venice were a box of chocolates, which would you choose? Imagine you are in Venice for only two hours. How would you spend your time?

Venice has always been a city of art. During the Renaissance,[9] it had its own school of painting. Artists like Bellini and Vivarini were interested in the relationship between color and light. Painters of that period made oil paint popular because it lasted a long time in the wet lagoon area. The use of these materials in the wet, Venetian climate helped create a new style full of rich colors. Tintoretto was one of the most famous Venetian painters of this time. His painting *Paradise*, which is one of the largest paintings of its kind, is an example of this style of art.

[9]**Renaissance:** a time of change in art, literature, and ideas in 15th- and 16th-century Europe

Wood, stone, and glass were also used to make many wonderful things. In fact, by the 12th century, glass making was one of the most important businesses in Venice. In the 13th century, glass makers were told to move from the city center to another island called Murano.

There are two possible reasons for this. Firstly, civic leaders said they were afraid that fire from the glass factories could destroy the wooden buildings of the city. Secondly, if the glass was made on an island, nobody could find out the secret of how to make it.

Many people believe that the second reason was more important. In fact, some years later, glass makers were not allowed to leave the island at all. Today, Murano glass is still famous, and you can visit the island and see how it is made.

Antonio Vivaldi

Venice is also a musical city. During the Renaissance, musicians traveled from all over Europe to study there. It was one of the first cities to start printing music as well. Venice's most famous composer is probably Antonio Vivaldi. He spent almost 40 years working on his music at the church of *Santa Maria della Pietá*. This church was home to many poor young girls who had no families. Vivaldi taught them to sing and play musical instruments. Some of the musical instruments he bought for them are still on display in the church today.

You can also find Venice in many different works of art.

Shakespeare's plays *Othello* and *The Merchant of Venice* take place there.

And with its spectacular beauty, it is no surprise that Venice is the star of many movies, too.

February is carnival time, and during *carnevale*, Venice is one big party! Carnival first began at the end of the 13th century as a religious celebration. Forty days before Easter,[10] people stopped eating meat. Carnevale means "goodbye to meat." Before beginning 40 days without meat, the people of Venice organized a meat-eating festival. They dressed in colorful costumes and hid their faces behind masks. Today, many people still wear costumes and cover their faces, and Venetian masks are famous all over the world.

[10] **Easter:** a Christian holiday in March or April

Video Quest

Carnevale!

Watch this video to learn more about the Carnival of Venice. How long does it last? What do people do during the day? What happens at night?

CHAPTER 4

The Future of Venice

THE FIRST VENETIANS CHOSE TO MAKE THE LAGOON THEIR HOME BECAUSE IT WAS SAFE. NOW, BECAUSE OF ITS GEOGRAPHY, VENICE IS IN DANGER.

Sixteen hundred years ago, the sea was almost two meters lower than it is now. Venetians had to walk up steps from the boats into their houses. But now, partly because of global warming,[11] the water in the lagoon is rising.

But it is not only the rising water that is putting Venice in danger. Venice itself is sinking. Over the years, the wooden piles that Venice is built on have sunk deeper into the ground.

....

[11]**global warming:** an increase in the temperature around the world caused by pollution

In the 20th century, Venetians began building wells[12] to get fresh water. This reduced the amount of water deep underground, making Venice sink even more quickly. Since the 1960s, the building of wells hasn't been allowed. Fortunately, it seems that the sinking of the city is slowing down.

In late fall and winter, there is more wind and rain. This is the time of the *acqua alta*, or "high water." The sea enters the lagoon from the Adriatic and floods many areas of the city. The worst flood was in 1966. The water was almost two meters higher in some parts of the city. Venice was in danger of being destroyed.

[12]**well:** a deep hole in the ground where you can get water

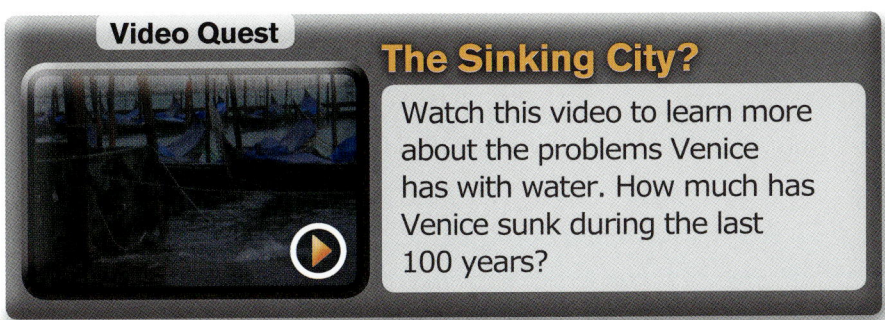

Video Quest

The Sinking City?

Watch this video to learn more about the problems Venice has with water. How much has Venice sunk during the last 100 years?

For some years, there has been a plan to stop the floods. The idea is to build 79 gates between the lagoon and the Adriatic Sea. These gates would usually be full of water at the bottom of the sea. However, during the Acqua Alta, they would fill up with air. This would make them float to the top of the sea. Then they would stop the water from entering the lagoon.

But there are problems with the plan. Some say it would be bad for the environment. Sea water wouldn't go in and out of the lagoon in a natural way. This would be dangerous for sea life, and dirty water would not be taken out of the city. This might mean that people could not live in Venice anymore. The plan is also extremely expensive. Can civic organizations or the Italian government really spend $4 billion to save Venice from the sea? Venetians hope so, but for the moment, they are still waiting.

Tourism can also be a big problem for Venice. It has 50,000 visitors a day, which makes it overcrowded. And many tourists only visit Venice for a day. They arrive on cruise ships or buses, see the sights quickly, and spend very little money on hotels or restaurants. So Venice gets the crowds but not the money!

At the same time that tourism is rising, Venice's normal population is getting smaller. In 2009, there were just under 60,000 residents.[13] That is 60 percent fewer people than in 1952. Many Venetians simply can't afford to buy homes there anymore. Some Italians fear that Venice is becoming a "living museum," or a historical Disneyland.

[13] **resident:** a person who normally lives in a place

Traffic on the canals is also a problem. There are big "truck" boats and small passenger boats. There are even ambulance boats to take sick people to hospital! This means traffic jams and a lot of pollution. Cruise ships often sail into the center of Venice. They make big waves, and this water movement damages[14] the buildings.

Garbage is a problem in Venice, too. People leave it outside in plastic bags, and then workers collect it at night. They take it to big green boats on the canals.

[14]**damage:** hurt something or make it look bad

But birds often get there first. They break the bags and the wind carries the garbage around the city. A lot of it ends up floating in the canals. And canals are difficult things to clean!

Venetians have talked about trying to control tourism. They already sell special tickets so visitors don't have to wait in line at every tourist sight, but that's not enough. Perhaps visitors could check the number of crowds in Venice on the Internet before they decide to go there. Cruise ships may not be allowed to sail into the city center in the future. But one thing is certain: Venice is in danger.

?

EVALUATE

What should Venice do about its tourist problem? Should all visitors have to pay to enter the city? Should they allow only a certain number of tourists every month?

After You Read

Read the following sentences and choose Ⓐ, Ⓑ, or Ⓒ.

1 In the 5th century, people chose to live in the Venetian lagoon area because it _____ .

Ⓐ was very beautiful
Ⓑ had a very big port
Ⓒ was safe

2 The people of Venice had made a lot of money by the 13th century because of _____ .

Ⓐ the power of the church
Ⓑ international trade
Ⓒ their political ideas

3 The piles under Venetian buildings have lasted a long time because they are _____ .

Ⓐ in sea water
Ⓑ next to rocks
Ⓒ made of stone

4 In 17th-century Venice, gondolas were _____ .

Ⓐ useful
Ⓑ beautiful
Ⓒ expensive

5 Tintoretto was one of the most famous _____ during the Renaissance.

Ⓐ painters
Ⓑ architects
Ⓒ glass makers

6 Venetian glass makers had to _____ .

Ⓐ leave the center of Venice
Ⓑ sell their glass very cheaply
Ⓒ destroy all their factories

7 Today, the buildings in Venice are too _____ .

    Ⓐ old

    Ⓑ low

    Ⓒ high

8 Many Venetians are leaving the city because it's too _____ .

    Ⓐ polluted

    Ⓑ crowded

    Ⓒ expensive

Complete the Text

Write one word in each space.

Venice is built in a **❶** _____ near the Adriatic Sea. This means there is water everywhere. People often travel around the city by boats that sail along the many **❷** _____ . When the weather is bad, there are **❸** _____ , especially in the lowest parts of the city. Some people have thought about how to stop this happening. The plan is to build 79 **❹** _____ so that sea water can't enter the city. This plan is very **❺** _____ , though, so Venetians must wait to see what happens.

❓ ANALYZE

Write three things about Venice in the first column below. Now think about the city or town where you live. How is it similar / different to Venice? Put a check mark (√) in the correct column. Then write an article comparing your city with Venice. Where would you prefer to live?

Venice	My city is similar	My city is different

Answer Key

Words to Know, page 4

1 flood **2** palace **3** costume **4** mask **5** lagoon

Words to Know, page 5

1 trade **2** float **3** carnival **4** decorate **5** rise

Analyze, page 4
Answers will vary.

Video Quest, page 7
Venice was built on wood that was sunk into the lagoon. People use canals to get around the city by boat. From the Grand Canal, people can see historical buildings.

Analyze, page 11
Answers will vary.

Apply, page 15
Answers will vary.

Video Quest, page 19
The Carnival lasts more than two weeks. During the day, people walk through the square in colorful costumes and wear masks. At night, there are parties and fireworks.

Video Quest, page 21
Venice has sunk 24 centimeters in the last 100 years.

Evaluate, page 25
Answers will vary.

Choose the Correct Answers, page 26

1 C **2** B **3** A **4** B **5** A **6** A **7** B **8** C

Complete the Text, page 27

1 lagoon **2** canals **3** floods **4** gates **5** expensive

Analyze, page 28
Answers will vary.